A Princess FOREVER

Reflecting the Fruit of the Spirit as a Daughter of The King

CHERYL DELAMARTER

Acknowledgements

A big thank you to Bruce DeRoos with Left Coast Design whose designs captured the vision I had in creating this book, a treasure to be enjoyed by girls of all ages.

FIRST SILVER THREAD PUBLISHING EDITION, NOVEMBER 2017

All rights reserved. No part of this book may be reproduced, scanned, or distributed in any printed or electronic form without explicit written permission. Please do not participate in or encourage piracy of copyrighted materials in violation of the author's rights.

Silver Thread Publishing is a division of A Silver Thread, Pismo Beach, CA

www.asilverthread.com

Copyright © 2016 by Cheryl Delamarter

Cover and Interior Design by Left Coast Design, Portland, OR

ISBN 978-0-999179420

Printed in the United States of America

Dedication

This book
is dedicated to my
precious granddaughters
and to all young ladies who
come to Jesus as their Lord and
Savior, becoming a princess
forever as a daughter
of The King!

Introduction

Girls dream of becoming princesses dressed in elegance, reflecting a beauty so rare. One may dress up and follow all the mannerisms of a princess, yet unless daughter of a king, she can never become a princess at all! As we look back thousands of years to the greatest historical event in time, we find the key that transforms any girl into a true princess, forever, as a daughter of The King!

Jesus, God in the flesh, came to earth to set hearts and lives free from sin and death. Through his death and resurrection, Jesus took the punishment for sin, so that his children, wrapped in a garment of salvation, can be forgiven, cleansed and redeemed for his kingdom, a life everlasting.

As the gift of the incomprehensible love of Jesus is embraced and the heart surrendered to Him, a girl becomes a child of THE KING, a true princess.

Clothed in a robe of righteousness, (Isaiah 61:10), this princess is on a journey that begins the transformation process of developing a heart and actions to be more like Jesus!

Once a daughter of King Jesus, the Holy Spirit dwells within as Counselor. (John 14:16) He convicts when there is wrong doing to encourage confession of sins, making lives right once again. He also intercedes and reminds that Jesus' love is always and forever! He will never leave nor forsake his children! (Hebrews 13:5)

As his daughter nurtures her love for Jesus, spending time in his Holy Word, the Bible, and in prayer, the Fruit of the Spirit begins to grow within: love, joy, peace, patience, kindness, goodness, faithfulness, gentleness, and self-control. (Galatians 5:22-23) Turn the pages to visit the life changing Fruit of the Spirit and how these delightful traits shine through to others in daily living as a true princess of The King!

The Holy Spirit dwells within,

So the fruit of the Spirit may grow

To touch a heart

And bless a life,

Dear princess, you must know!

Delight your heart daily

Sharing the fruit:

Love, joy, peace, patience,
Kindness, goodness too,

Faithfulness, gentleness,
and self-control,

Actions that shine
to influence all

Love

Choose to love Jesus with all of your heart!
Love others, whether or not it's deserved
Practice acts of kindness
Showing love by your actions,
Not just by your words

For love is the greatest gift
One we should freely give
Knowing King Jesus loved you first*
Bless others
By the way you live

But the greatest of these is love.
I Corinthians 13:13b NIV

*I John 4:19

Joy

Sing praise to Jesus with a joyful heart!
Adore, worship, and revere Him
In everything, give thanks
Trusting God to work
All things together for your good*

When you pray
Thank Jesus before He answers
Let the joy in your heart overflow
Help others to see
That your greatest joy
Is found in loving Jesus

Shout with joy to God, all the earth! Sing the glory of his name; make his praise glorious!

Psalm 66:1-2 NIV

*Romans 8:28

Peace

Strive to live at peace with all
Do not pick quarrels or fights,
Try to understand people
Not determined to always be right

Respond with loving-kindness
Listen before you speak
Consider others before yourself
Let your heart be filled with peace

If it is possible, as far as it depends on you,
live at peace with everyone.
ROMANS 12:18 NIV

Patience

Wait on God; practice patience
HIS timing is oh so perfect
Pray with thanksgiving
Trusting God
For He knows for you, what is best!

Be patient with others
As Jesus with you,
Your mishaps and wrongs, forgiven
As Jesus forgives completely,
You must forgive others too!

Therefore, as God's chosen people, holy and dearly loved, clothe yourselves with compassion, kindness, humility, gentleness and patience. Bear with each other and forgive whatever grievances you may have against one another.

COLOSSIANS 3:12-13 NIV

Kindness

A heart in love with Jesus
Grows in kindness everyday
Not intending to hurt,
Rather, to bless,
Forever and always

Consider others' feelings
Before your very own
Being ever so mindful
To show kindness to others,
For you WILL reap what you sow*

Be kind and compassionate to one another,
forgiving each other, just as in Christ God forgave you.

EPHESIANS 4:32 NIV

* Galatians 6:7

Goodness

Be good!
Obey God's commands
Obey your parents too*
Your heart will grow in goodness
Living to do well toward others,
Just as you would have them do to you**

Let us not become weary in doing good,
for at the proper time we will reap
a harvest if we do not give up.
GALATIANS 6:9 NIV

*Ephesians 6:1
**Matthew 7:12

Faithfulness

Oh, do be faithful to Jesus!
Spend time with Him everyday
In his Word and in prayer
Knowing him better,
Loving him deeper
Living life with care

Be faithful to others,
A child of your word;
Honest, responsible, and true
A princess of integrity,
One to be trusted,
Loved, and admired too

Let love and faithfulness never leave you; bind them around your neck, write them on the tablet of your heart.

PROVERBS 3:3 NIV

Gentleness

Remember, all God's children
Are brought into the world with purpose
Be gentle, do be kind,
Even when thoughts and actions
Differ from yours at times

Show respect to all people
Even when undeserved
Reflect the love of Jesus
Keeping your commitment to Him
Without reserve!

Let your gentleness be evident to all. The Lord is near.

PHILIPPIANS 4:5 NIV

Self Control

Practice self-control
Keep your feelings and emotions in check
Do not be angry or gossip
Think before you speak and act

Be strong
Say, "No!" to things that can sway you
From all that is right and good
Practice self-control
Doing all things as you should!

For the grace of God... teaches us to say "No" to ungodliness and worldly passions, and to live self-controlled, upright and godly lives in this present age...
TITUS 2:11-12 NIV

As your beauty reflects
The Fruit of the Spirit
Bask in the blessings
Each trait will bring,

A life well lived
Faithful and true
A daughter,
A princess of The King!

Bibliography

Life Application Study Bible, New International Version. Wheaton: Zondervan Publishing House, 2005

Illustrations

Cover image, Dedication Page: Copyright: StudioLondon, Shutterstock.com
Page 9, 10, 20, 28: Copyright: Pushkin, Shutterstock.com
Page 12: Copyright: Copyright: ayelet-keshet, , Shutterstock.com
Page 14, 16, 22, 24, 30: Copyright: Azuzl, Shutterstock.com
Page 18, Copyright: Anastacia - azzzya, Shutterstock.com
Page 26, Copyright: artbesouro, Shutterstock.com
Page 32, Copyright: Jacky Brown, Shutterstock.com

www.ingramcontent.com/pod-product-compliance
Lightning Source LLC
Chambersburg PA
CBHW041128300426
44113CB00003B/93